I0772663

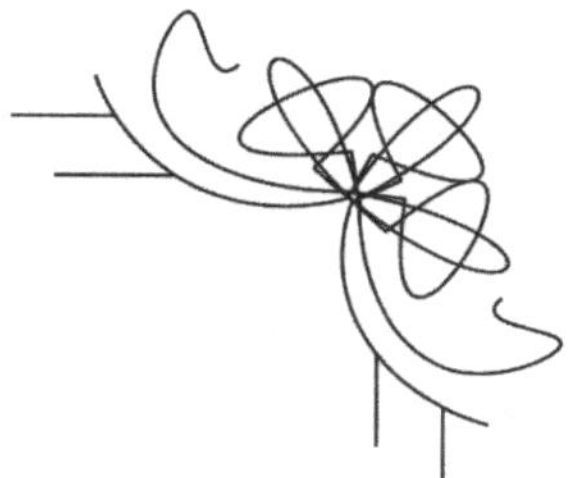

This Coloring Book Belongs To:

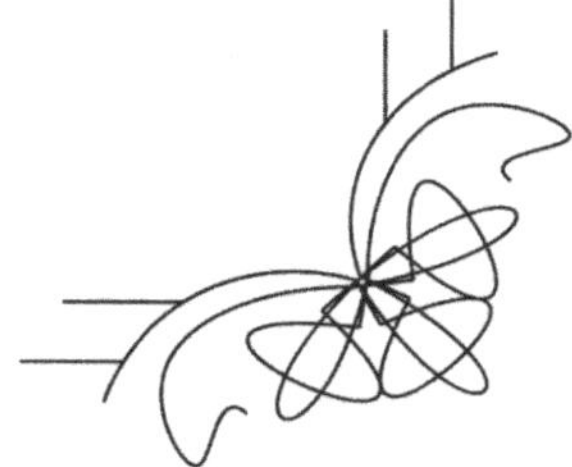

DREAM LIKE A UNICORN

COLORING BOOK

COLORING BOOK

COLORING BOOK

COLORING BOOK

COLORING BOOK

COLORING BOOK

COLORING BOOK

COLORING BOOK 

COLORING BOOK

COLORING BOOK

COLORING BOOK

coffee

COLORING BOOK

COLORING BOOK

COLORING BOOK

COLORING BOOK

COLORING BOOK

COLORING BOOK

COLORING BOOK

COLORING BOOK

COLORING BOOK

COLORING BOOK

COLORING BOOK

COLORING BOOK

COLORING BOOK 

COLORING BOOK

COLORING BOOK

COLORING BOOK

COLORING BOOK

COLORING BOOK

COLORING BOOK 

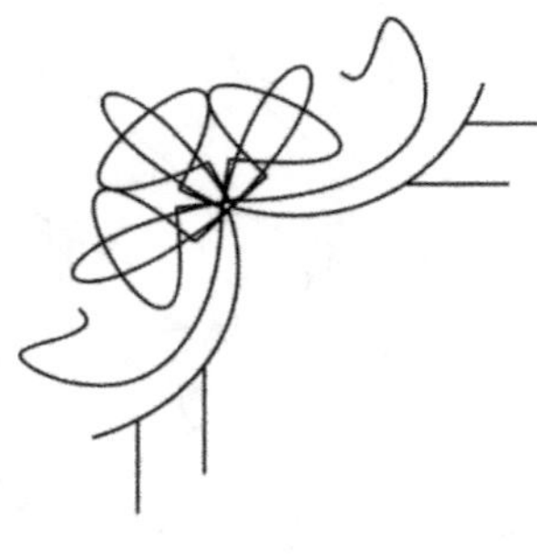

Copyright © 2020

All rights reserved. No part of this publication
may be reproduced, distributed, or transmitted
in any form or by any means, including
photocopying, recording, or other electronic or
mechanical methods, without the prior written
permission of the publisher, except
in the case of brief quotations embodied
in critical reviews and certain other
noncommercial uses permitted by copyright law

www.ingramcontent.com/pod-product-compliance
Lightning Source LLC
Chambersburg PA
CBHW081320250726
48662CB00008B/2660